MOKI'S

REVENGE

A Polo
Legacy

By MOKI
Co-authors Fred Dailey & P.T. Brent

FIRST PRINTING 04 JULY 2024

© 2024 by P. T. Brent

ISBN: 9798328517775

PUBLISHERS NOTE

Printed in the United States.

A TRIBUTE ... to Fred and Murph Dailey

04 July 2024   Repeating the SALUTE

A SALUTE ... to Fred and Murph Dailey

Originally written 17 March 2013

FLASHBACK HAWAII 1975 ... Arriving in Hawaii in 1975, this scribe was clearly a "rookie/non" poloist. With the desire to witness this sport and an invitation in hand from Fred Dailey to visit the Hawaii Polo Club at Mokuleia, it was time to meet two of the polo world's most exceptional people - Murph and Fred Dailey.

My first visit to the Hawaii Polo Club, aka "Moki's Polo Club," launched my long-term passion for the game. Fred and Murph Dailey were the epitome of style and class on and off the polo field. My inaugural chucker on the side field was played against Murph Dailey. She easily won the game and rode away with my heart forever!

Murph Dailey's genuine concern for people, coupled with Fred Dailey's ineluctable energy, passion for tradition, and above all, sense of humor, created a polo legacy second to none during the latter half of the twentieth century. To echo a sentiment from Bob MacGregor, another polo legend, *"In Hawaii, Fred Dailey is clearly MISTER POLO."*

A few years and many polo experiences later, Fred invited this, then less gifted, writer to stay in his lagoon apartment in Waikiki to help edit his biography along with his secretary, Blanche-an experience that once again offered testimony to "America's greatest generation." The resulting book entitled "MEMORIES 1908-1984" is an account of a wonderful life story. By the time you finish reading it, you will fall in love with Fred, Murph and their lovely family. WHY NOT? Everyone else does!

KYEOTB
P.T. Brent - Honolulu

MOKI'S REVENGE

BY
MOKI as told to FRED Dailey

Moki wants to tutor his mainland Haole visitors. My name is a nickname for Mokuleia Polo Farms located on a distant corner on the island of Oahu. Note: This is far as one can drive on island without their hat floating.

Haole (/ˈhaʊliː/; Hawaiian [ˈhɔule]) is a Hawaiian term for individuals who are not Native Hawaiian and is applied to people primarily of European ancestry.

MOKI'S CHALLENGE

Artist, DAN FOWLER, a.k.a. heckler, a movie maker, freezer, and one cool guy, has masterfully hidden 7 secrets from the Dailey family life on the front cover.
CAN YOU FIND ALL SEVEN?

There may be a hint somewhere later in this book!

Mokuleia Polo Farm   1 May 1990

Aloha Friends,

Moki was going to write another book for publication but due to the sad event guess I will pass it up. Sadly, Henry Lyons is no longer with us.

Henry was the guy that did all those wonderful cartoons in my book, Polo Is A Four Letter Word" and he was my good friend. Although he didn't play polo he had a good life. He loved to eat, drink and have fun and still found time to be one of the greatest cartoonists of his time. I'm just glad I knew Henry and so will all of his old friends who` enjoyed his art.

In the meantime, here are some of the chapters I had already written, but they won't be as interesting without those great illustrations. Albeit we have challenged Dan Fowler, an artist of some repute, to follow in Henry's footsteps.

                                        Moki

Good news ... the new talent is, you will see, quite successful... Moki's Revenge.

TABLE OF CONTENTS

The last story in Fred's book is Moki's law

###############################

Co-author, P T Brent, experienced his first polo chucker riding me, Moki. It is fun to think I taught him everything about polo. These are some of his conversations with me.

ACCOLADES

Just finished Moki's Revenge...

Wonderful Patrick. Beautifully done.

Thank you for your thoughtfulness and humor.

Much enjoyed... but must admit

to being a bit teary eyed.....

Mahalos & Alohas!

Michael Dailey

MOKI'S

REVENGE

A Polo
Legacy

Dear Pasture Friends,
    Look at that – this human cannot spell NEIGH!
Just one more reason we need to be in charge.
                              Love,
                              MOKI

TRAINING DAZE

Last night, as we were standing in our pasture, my fellow horses and I started discussing the amusing antics of our human friends. It's quite comical, the assortment of metal contraptions they use to control us, labeling them as bits, curb reins, snaffle reins, and draw reins, as if we were some sort of mechanical contraption.

It seems they overlook the simple fact that if they raised and handled us properly, there would be no need for such devices in our mouths, except perhaps to counteract the bad habits they've inadvertently instilled in us. Throughout the ages, we've been loyal servants to humans, always eager to please and assist them. All we require is a bit of understanding and patience during our formative years, and we quickly grasp their desires.

The truth is, very few of us are inherently ill-tempered or vicious. If we appear dangerous or agitated when first ridden, it's likely because we're frightened and uncertain of what is expected from us. Our memories are sharp, and with a few gentle reminders about when to stop, go, turn, and respond to signals, we never forget.

The boss, whom I assume is the more experienced rider, shares insights about proper treatment with the younger players, attempting to instill a sense of respect and understanding. Unfortunately, there always seems to be a stubborn individual around, forcefully grabbing at the reins and treating us roughly.

This 'polo pony' (pull lop pa nee) often daydreams about what would happen if one of these humans experienced being bridled, bitted, and ridden like we are. It would be intriguing to see how they would handle it. Perhaps they'd gain a newfound appreciation for the patience and cooperation they expect from us.

And imagine the spectacle of a polo game where we horses swapped roles, gallivanting around the field, skillfully hitting the ball, while our human pals struggled to adapt down below. That would be quite a sight, wouldn't it?

DOLLARS AND SENSE $$$$

In the world of polo, where dollars and sense often collide, our protagonist (and my boss) had an enlightening moment. Faced with the challenge of being the weakest link in high-goal teams, he decided to take control of the situation.

Having owned four or five horses and playing among ten to twelve goal teams, he found himself overshadowed by more skilled players. Frustration reached its peak as he rarely got a chance to hit the ball; commands like "leave it" or "take the man" echoed around him, drowning his opportunities.

Driven by the desire for more playtime and less expenditure, he devised a plan. After a meticulous calculation of hits, expenses, and the overall cost of maintaining multiple horses, he arrived at a revelation. Each hit cost him about fifty bucks, a realization that prompted a change in strategy.

Our hero bid farewell to the high-stakes world of medium and high-goal polo. Now, armed with only two horses, he embraced low goal teams and beginners. This shift not only afforded him ample opportunities to strike the ball but also allowed him to take charge, guiding less experienced players with his shouts of "leave it."

In this new arena, he found not just the joy of the game but also significant savings.

Sir Winston Churchill, the storied prime minister
of the United Kingdom, once famously declared,
"polo is a passport to the world.".

Excerpt from Hawaiian Hospitality Magazine 1961

FRED DAILEY

"........Dailey, who was born in Aurora, Illinois constructed and operated resorts in Southern California. After opening the Waikikian in Hawaii, he also developed the Driftwood Hotel and the Mokuleia Beach Colony.

Organizer and president of the Hawaii Polo Club at Mokuleia, he has revived the sport that was once the fancy of King Kalakaua at Kapiolani Park. He is also a member of the Santa Barbara Polo Club and governor of the U.S. Polo Association and is instrumental in bringing clubs from Ireland, Britain (including Prince Charles), Chile, Florida, California, and the Philippines to highlight the five-month season."

POLO TRAVELS

In my conversations with the boss I sure learn a lot about polo around the world. He's played in England, Ireland, Spain, and in the Pacific, Far East and in places with some real funny names.

He says that most polo in the world is played like ours here in Hawaii, except for a couple of places I got to tell you about, like Tokyo, where his team played a game in the palace not long after the war was over. They played in an indoor ring and on riding horses that didn't know much about the game.

Also, the umpire walks instead of riding around, which didn't make much difference as the whole thing was a slow-motion scene. Anyway, they all had fun and plenty of 'Sake' after the game.

Then they played in Hong Kong on little Asian ponies used by the Gurka mountain troops. As these were all stallions there were a few bites and kicks here and there. The ponies were so small they used special shortened mallets, and our long-legged guys looked like they were dragging their feet when aboard. But those little studs were plenty tough and played a helluva game, which our guys lost as they'd had no practice with this miniature polo.

In a place called Kuala Lumpur they played on a field covered with water during a monsoon deluge. As the King of Malaysia, who also plays polo, was on hand to umpire, they just kept on playing while the skies dumped an ocean of rain on players and field. I guess the Malaysians were used to it, but our guys almost got drowned.

For several years, they'd go to Manila where polo was very popular with the Spanish and Filipinos. For some strange reason (maybe the horses they were loaned) they always lost the first game but managed a few wins in the second games.

They won the Irish Gold Cup in Dublin and tried to bring it back to Hawaii (it's solid gold), but the Irish cops said "No, it stays here. All you guys get is your names engraved on the trophy."

HORSERADISH

HORSE  PLAY

FEELING HORSEY?

Originally written by Fred Dailey... A whimsical and humorous view of the polo and horse world.

Well, well, if it isn't us horses getting all the credit and blame in the world. They've got us tied to more things than we've got horseshoes! Let's take a lighthearted trot through this equine world of fame and infamy:

- **Horseradish:** We're like the spice of the vegetable kingdom - good and strong. They named it after us because we're just that impactful.
- **Horse-Latitudes:** Not the calmest weather-wise, but hey, we like to keep things interesting. No snoozefest when we're around.
- **Horsepower:** Ever wondered why those smelly old cars can't run without us? We're the real driving force, quite literally.
- **Year of the Horse:** Even the Chinese calendar agrees, every now and then it's our time to shine. Luck follows us like a tail.
- **Horseshoes:** Can't be lucky without them. It's like our four-leaf clover, but in metal form.
- **Horse Cavalry:** Tanks and helicopters might be cool, but there's something timeless about a cavalry on horseback. We paved the way before the mechanical invasion!
- **Horseplay, Horselaugh, Horsehair, Horse manure:** They've associated us with everything, even the messy stuff. But hey, that's life in the barn.
- **Horsewhipping:** Now, that's something I'd like to see done to some of our riders. A gentle nudge to keep them in line, perhaps?

And who knows, maybe all of this is just a horse of a different color. Life is never dull when you've got a hoof in every aspect of it.

The Welsh Corgi is a small type of herding dog that originated in Wales. The name corgi is derived from the Welsh words cor and ci, meaning "dwarf" and "dog", respectively.

KIWI

Our dear friend Kiwi is no longer here to bark at us and have fun making believe she's bossing us around. Moki guesses she's gone to that big pasture up in the sky where we'll all see her again someday.

Maybe we shouldn't feel so bad, for Kiwi had a long life with us and with her polo friends. She was almost fifteen years old and that's old for a Corgi. According to the way humans reckon their age she'd be over ninety.

In the last year or so Kiwi was sleeping a lot and having a hard time getting around. Maybe she was hurting from what they call arthritis, although she never told us and she was always her sweet and lovable self.

What happened was one day when Murph and the boss were on the mainland, she just didn't show up for dinner, and when Mike and Mark looked for her, they found her curled up by the pasture fence where I guess her heart just stopped.

When I told the boss he took it well, and later I guess he broke the news as gently as he could to Murph.

Mike showed them where he had buried **Kiwi** in a comer of our pasture where she could be near us and near the ocean where she loved to sit and watch the waves. There's a stone to remind us of a friend we dearly miss, and who we all look forward to seeing again someday.

Look into my eyes.
Listen to my heart.
I will give you everything,
Until my strength departs.

My trust in you complete.
I feel what you are thinking,
Every movement a message.
Our connection interlinking.

I follow where you lead,
I ask nothing but your care.
My Shadow is your Shadow,
My back will take you anywhere.

Don't Cry For The Horses

by Brenda Riley-Seymore

Don't cry for the horses that life has set free.
A million white horses forever to be.
Don't cry for the horses now in God's hand.
As they dance and they prance in a heavenly band.
They were ours as a gift, but never to keep.
As they close their eyes forever to sleep.
Their spirits unbound. On silver wings they fly.
A million white horses against the blue sky.
Look up into heaven, you'll see them above.
The horses we lost, the horses we loved.
Manes and tails flowing they gallop through time.
They were never yours - they were never mine.
Don't cry for the horses. They'll be back someday.
When our time is gone, they will show us the way.
Do you hear that soft nicker? Close to your ear?
Don't cry for the horses. Love the ones that are here.

KAHILI

Last Sunday one of my friends had an accident and busted a leg during the polo game. It was just one of those crazy things that happen when you least expect it. Kahili was playing her usual great game and doing one of those famous speed-turns like only she can, and something just gave way.

Her friends gathered round, and the Vet came and Mike who was playing her was crying, and didn't want to finish the game, but the boss insisted and so the crowd of fans never knew how seriously Kahili was hurt.

Well, they loaded her on a truck and took her over to the mountain pasture where they said goodbye to her under a lovely green Ironwood tree. She didn't seem to feel any pain although the leg was badly broken, and the Vet said there was no way to save her.

The boss gave her some green sprigs to chew on and rubbed her gums with his finger like he used to do when she was a baby and told her again how much he and Mike and all her friends loved her. Then the Vet gave her a quick injection she didn't feel, and she went to sleep. The boss was going to untie her tail but decided she should be buried in all her beauty, ready and prepared for the game as the great polo pony she was.

Moki is informed that there's a Supreme Umpire up there in the sky. He's in charge of all the polo fields and the beautiful pastures where all of us are gonna meet some day. Well, I can just see Kahili up there now. With that great heart and all that speed, I'll bet she's making plenty of goals for her rider.

WHO'S GOT THE COOKIES?

Here come the San Franciscans again, flaunting their pink shirts with determination to secure a victory this year, especially after the tied score against our local team last season.

Personally, I'm rooting for them, mainly because the Irish Captain of the S.F. team is in the cookie business, and you know how much Moki adores anything related to apples or cookies. Of course, Moki can't express my sentiments to Murph, given her enthusiastic cheers for Mike when he plays against the S.F.'s for the home team.

The boss had mentioned the possibility of loaning Moki to the San Francisco team for a chukker, but I suppose I might be a tad too seasoned for such a high-speed game. Nevertheless, I was saddled up and ready, just in case they needed my seasoned expertise.

Well, on Sunday, much to my surprise and contrary to my usual horse sense, the S.F.'s outplayed our team, leaving them with their mallets hanging out. In the first chukker, those pink-shirted competitors knocked in a couple of goals, and as the game progressed, they continued their scoring spree, while our team seemed to struggle in the saddle.

The final score stood at 7 to 4 in favor of the visitors, earning them the privilege of indulging in the champagne celebration after the game. As for me, I made a beeline for the barn in the hopes of discovering where they stashed those elusive cookies. Unfortunately, my search was fruitless, but Murph generously shared a couple with me later, acknowledging the sacrifice it was for her to part with them.

Looking ahead, Moki sincerely hopes that when the San Francisco's return next year, the cookie connoisseur remembers our connection. I have a feeling he will, considering I allowed him to ride me in his inaugural polo game. While I may not be as swift as I once was, I've become a discerning judge of oats, apples, and, you guessed it, Laura Todd Cookies.

Not who, but what should rule society? **That should be Morality, Integrity, and Truth.** We have seen, over and over again, that people are not fit to rule other people. This mentality is what creates psychopathic behavior within the rulers. Like the famous quote *"power corrupts and absolute power corrupts absolutely"*.

<u>So why would we continue putting people</u>

<u>in charge to rule?</u>

TIME for the PONIES to SET THE RULES

"It took Moki a good while to grasp all the peculiar nuances that constitute a polo game.

Consider this: when a player hoists his mallet into the air, it's not an urgent bathroom call; rather, it's his way of signaling to the umpire that the fellow in front committed a foul. Corky Linfoot will even call a foul on a player that is appealing for a foul when he's waving a mallet or giving a 'mean stare' at the umpire. A 'mean stare" is called a 'stink eye' in the Sandwich Isles.

Most umpires pay little mind to these mallet-waving antics, yet the players persist. Some creatures with two legs just can't lose a game without lamenting that they've been 'robbed.' These chaps likely began bellowing about life's unfairness when they first drew breath without a bottle in hand.

Here's another irksome bit – when the umpire blows the whistle on my rider for rough riding just as I've concluded imparting a sound thump to one of those haughty visiting ponies, hoping to impart a lesson.

It's a pity they don't let us ponies set the rules. We'd surely straighten out a few of those players and their ponies as well.

TEXAS

And there was the team from Texas, with their big hats.

These guys were all pretty big and darn good players too. Most of them were brought up on ranches and knew plenty about horses.

They were all nice gentlemen although there were a lot of jokes about Texas, and oil wells, and how big they were and about Texans who put ketchup on pie and even on their steaks.

But they didn't let anything bother them and just went along and tramped all over our guys winning the big game by a bunch of goals.

When somebody told one of the Texas guys Moki was a well-broken filly, he said "Hell mister, that there pony ain't even bent. She's just as good as any gol-damed horse that ever came out of the great state of Texas".

So you can see why I'm kind of partial to Texans.

FATSO

Some of these so-called equestrians give me a pain in what is known to the more vulgar as my fanny.

Like the big fat broad who marches around in tight britches and boots and carries a whip.

Moki had a chat with her pony and this is what he said: "It ain't so bad being owned by old fatso. She feeds me almost as well, as she feeds herself. Although it's quite a load when she climbs on my back, she doesn't let me go much faster than a trot so I don't have to work very hard. And that whip is only for show. She only used it on me once and the moment I felt it I took off like a shot and left her lying on the turf, which didn't hurt her much with all that padding she's got."

Anyway, Moki feels kind of sorry for her for I think she only hangs around with us horses to keep an eye on that husband of hers. He's that skinny polo playing character with an eye for the gals.

Maybe if she'd take off some of that excess she wouldn't have to wear those tight pants and make believe she's a horsewoman just to keep that guy of hers in line.

CHOW

Well, folks, The Boss and Murph just sailed back from a fancy boat trip to China, so it looks like the menu around here is changing to Chop Suey. Beats the heck out of those hay cubes we've been munching on. Those cubes are like crunchy tooth traps—thanks to some farmer in California with too much time on his hands. He took old hay, squashed it into hard little cubes, and voila, a dental dilemma for us horses. I swear, they're seasoned with the flavors of every weed and a hint of pasture mayo left by the previous horse tenants.

Living the Hawaiian life has its quirks. We don't get the fancy stuff California horses do. Hawaii's all about that cash economy with sugar, pineapples, and tourists. But seriously, who wants to chomp down on tourists or deal with the sugary consequences? So, yeah, we import our horse grub from the mainland, and I won't pretend to be thrilled about it.

Maybe one day, some horse-feeding genius will come up with a tastier solution. But until then, while The Boss and Murph enjoy their Chop Suey, I'll be here, nibbling away on these darn hay cubes. Cheers to the crunchy life!

Logo for Donegal Farms, Indio, CA. created by the
artist, the late, **ALEJANDRO MOY** of Argentina.

THE MONOGRAM

Ever notice those high-priced shirts and all that fancy gear with those peculiar monograms? You know, like the one guy perched on something resembling a horse, casually brandishing a mallet in the air as if it were an ice cream cone?

Curious, I inquired of the boss why he didn't indulge in such elaborate shirts. He replied, "Moki, the folks sporting miniature animals on their attire, perhaps even on their pants, are akin to polo ponies incapable of engaging in a match without the adornment of a sophisticated saddle on their backs."

A salute to Polo Fashions founder Ralph Lifshitz
Why did Ralph Lauren change his name?

At age 16, he legally changed his second name from Lifshitz to Lauren along with his brother George Poitras Lauren, due to bullying at school. His choice of the name followed his older brother Jerry Lauren, who had first done so after experiencing bullying in the U.S. Air Force.

Moki believes this may be a 'special' story…

Doc simply reveled in the spirit of polo.

We cherished him as much as he did

the sport, and his absence will be

keenly felt.

GOOD-BYE BILL

It's a somber day at the Polo Club. We bid adieu to a dear friend.

All of us, the four-legged comrades, and those two-legged riders who guide us, will feel the absence of Doctor Bill. He was the man always present when those foolish polo players blundered, falling off their horses or colliding with a polo mallet.

Doc mended countless players throughout the years he spent with us. Remarkably, he never handed them a bill. Doc simply reveled in the spirit of polo. We cherished him as much as he did the sport, and his absence will be keenly felt. We imagine him now, up there, tending to players on that grand polo field. Someday, we'll reunite with him in that vast expanse.

Goodbye, Bill

HORSE SENSE?

Seems like folks are always turning to us humble horses to add a touch of flair to their conversations. So, I enlisted the boss to dig up some horse quotes and the clever minds behind them. Here's what he secured:

- A horse, a horse, my kingdom for a horse... (Shakespeare)
- Beggars mounted run their horses to death... (Shakespeare)
- Boots, saddle, to horse and away... (Refrain)
- A man may bring a horse to water but he cannot make him drink... (George Herbert 1640)
- Like the forced gait of a shuffling nag... (Pliny)
- Set the cart before the horse... (Shakespeare)
- In the choice of a horse or a wife, a man must please himself... (Melville)
- A dark horse rushing past the grandstand in sweeping triumph... (Disraeli)
- It's the difference of opinion that makes horse races... (Mark Twain)
- The horse, the symbol of surging potency and the canal of movement... (Apocalypse)

- Ride a cock horse to Banbury Cross, to see a fine lady on a white horse... (Anonymous)
- For want of a nail, the shoe is lost. For want of a shoe, the horse is lost. For want of a horse, the rider is lost... (Herbert)
- The horse knows the way to carry the sleigh... (child)
- Never look a gift horse in the mouth... (St. Jerome)
- Sit a beggar on horseback and he will ride at a gallop... (Shakespeare)
- All the king's horses and all the king's men, couldn't put Humpty Dumpty together again... (??)
- God forbid that I should go to any heaven in which there are no horses... (Theodore Roosevelt)
- If wishes were horses, beggars might ride... (Ray)
- It is best not to swap horses when crossing a stream... (A. Lincoln)
- A short horse is soon curried... (Haywood)
- When the steed is stolen, shut the stable door... (unknown)
- Us horses like us horses too... (Moki)

" There's nothing wrong with you that a little Prozac and a polo mallet can't cure."

...

Woody Allen

TRADITION OR CONFUSION

The boss has been on a mission for years, trying to convince the Polo Association to reconsider the rule about goal changes. According to the rule book, after a goal is scored, the game's direction is meant to switch. Supposedly, this quirky tradition originated in the early days of polo when some sage believed it would level the playing field, particularly considering the capricious winds.

None of us, players included, can fathom the logic behind this, especially when there's an equal number of periods in the game. The only conceivable advantage might be for the team winning the toss to determine which goal they start with, akin to football and tennis.

After a considerable uproar from players and spectators alike, who found themselves befuddled (and occasionally playing in the wrong direction), a compromise was attempted. The decision was made to switch goals for every chukker, providing a respite from the confusion. Many players and spectators welcomed this change, appreciating its simplicity. However, it seems that the allure of common sense was too straightforward.

Enter the naysayers, those stubborn traditionalists, who raised a clamor about preserving the sanctity of tradition. They staunchly refused to play any way but the old way. In the end, the U.S.P.A., in their wisdom (or perhaps yielding to the loudest voices), reverted to the original rule.

And so, the confusion persists, baffling everyone except the polo experts, who alone discern the game's elusive direction. To add a touch of irony, I, too, find myself occasionally veering in the wrong direction.

**Note: A Nine Goaler, once Governor,
failed on this mission long ago.**

PROBLEMS - BOOZE

"So, the other day, a predicament emerged.

One of our polo comrades, generally an amiable fellow, showed up for a match, and, goodness, he was thoroughly inebriated!

Now, our game is perilous even when our companions possess their full faculties. Though I'm no tattletale, nor an informant by nature, a sense of responsibility nudged me to act.

Before the umpire initiated the match, I called out to him to avert trouble before it unfolded. Yet, he was one of those who couldn't comprehend our language, so I dashed towards the sidelines to locate the boss.

The boss raced onto the field, brought everything to a standstill, caught a whiff of our friend's barley-laden breath, and promptly escorted him off the field. A replacement joined the game, and once it concluded, all the players convened for a meeting.

The outcome was that our imbibing comrade received a suspension from the club for the next month – no polo, no riding.

Perhaps now he'll opt for water, much like Moki does."

THE
QUESTION?

Well, Moki reckons it's a peculiar world indeed.

Horses like us, we don't have to worry 'bout those human troubles. We're just out there on the polo field, giving our riders a good run and helping them with that polo ball.

No need for the human vices like sniffing coke or drowning sorrows in booze. Life's simple for us, and I reckon it's a darn good one.

"Playing polo is like trying to play golf during an earthquake." ....

Sylvester Stallone

HAVE A LOUSY DAY

Guess the Boss is getting older and finding it harder to get along with his two-legged friends. But he still talks to me and tells me his troubles. He says he is so damn sick of being told to "have a nice day" that he is about to present the next guy who tries to tell him what to do with a very nice nosebleed. After all, who the hell wants a nice day.

If it rains, let it rain, if it snows, let it snow, if someone kicks you, kick him back, and as far as all that keep smiling stuff is concerned, neither the Boss' face nor mine was built for smiling. If they were we'd both be walking upside-down.

Did you ever see one of those polo players with a smile on his face? When they are playing polo all they do is chase that ball, and you'd think that the vicious way they hit at it they are trying to kill something.

You think they're having a nice day ?

POO – POO'S

When the Boss and I are talking he gets the opportunity to bitch about some of his pet hates in his two-legged world.

So, the other day he is telling me about the cocktail parties he must go to, where, he says, he always must stand with a drink in his hand, talking to some fat old lady who talks about her diet, or some business genius who tells him about how much he made in the market day before yesterday. Then there are the others, all clustered together in one part of the room with drinks in hand and all talking at full speed until the decibels are so high no one hears what the hell the guy or gal is saying, and who cares anyway.

Then along comes a waitress carrying hunks of fish or shrimp and something called deviled egg, or a hunk of celery dipped in something that looks like it came from their kids' nursery. And a piece of cold liver wrapped in greasy bacon, held together with a toothpick, which is the only useful part of this famous delicacy. But you can't use the toothpick anyway, it ain't polite, so you have another drink and try to remember the name of the guy who's bending your ear with some memories of events you forgot but which he tells you both enjoyed together way back when.

So, the Boss says he eventually works his way around a circle so they know they were in attendance, pulling his wife along they sneak out the door and head for a known in the Islands as poo - poo's, and which in the Boss' opinion is a pretty good name for something that stinks. Anyway, they were on hand for the six to eight cocktail parties that everyone in Hawaii thinks they must give for their friends once a year to pay back for the one their friends gave to pay their social dues.

Well, it sounds like the Boss has had his fair share of those fancy cocktail parties, surrounded by folks chatting away about diets, market gains, and who knows what else. I can imagine it gets tiresome. And those so-called hors d'oeuvres, or as they call them in the Islands, poo-poos, don't seem to be winning any favors either. Cold liver  wrapped in greasy bacon? I reckon that's not everyone's cup of tea.

Now, it seems the Boss has a strategy – make the rounds, nod, and smile, then make a swift exit with the wife in tow, seeking solace in a good restaurant and a few slugs of quality scotch. Can't blame him for wanting to wash away the taste of those "poo-poos."

Seems like these cocktail parties are a social duty in Hawaii, a way to repay the favor and keep the social circles turning. But hey, not everyone's cut out for that scene, and it sounds like the Boss knows how to navigate it his own way.

The

POLO is a SPORT

If they have both amateurs and professionals in sports like football, baseball, and golf, why not in polo?

AMATEURS OR PROFESSIONALS

So, all our polo guys are screaming about the cost of horses, which has gone sky-high.

It seems that with professional players, more or less taking over the game, the demand for the best polo horses has increased. The sponsors of these guys seem to have more ego than sense (they've got plenty of dollars) and don't care what they pay as long as their team wins.

For example, last year some polo beginner practically busted up the horse market by paying two or three times the former price for ponies so he could put a team together to win the big tournament. He and other low-goal high-ego characters will pay anything for pros and horses to be on a winning team.

The Boss says all the more reason we should separate the sport and let the pros survive with their paychecks from sponsors and patrons and let the amateurs have fun with their trophy collections. If they have both amateurs and professionals in sports like football, baseball, and golf, why not in polo?

My boss, Fred, was in the tourism business: polo and hotels...

– always trying to teach us ponies and players some common etiquette.

How to Greet Visitors:

20+ Examples to Try in Your Destination

(This rule was just one of his favorites)

Commonality

Establishing commonalities with ... through your community members gives visitors something to connect with. A shared value, perception, or even voice can make your destination relatable and instill trust.

So, being a good pony, agreed to take our visitors letter. But without a personal secretary, it was not neatly typed. If you know polo it should be easy to understand........
If you do not, give it a try before you turn the page.

MOKI and the VISITOR

There are always visitors here. Last week another horse came to me for a short conversation. Told him about the book I was writing and he asked if he could write a story for the book, too. Wanting to be gracious to our guest, said yes... and this is his story... in pidgin!

Yesterday I go Mokuleia see one polo game.
Da buggas on horse hit one itty ball with big stick, no hit horse. Big crowd yall like hell when ball fly in goal post likke foot ball goal. Bugga who hit ball no fall off horse. Too bad, I like see fall off.
Call horse polo pony. No look likke pony but go like hell. Tail tied maybe so no can shit on field. Rider wear white pants maybe so no can shit on horse.
Umpire on horse wear stripe shirt likke in jail and blow whistle. Stop game too damn much. I like shove whistle up umpire okole. When make goal all players go wrong way. Haoles all get excited up. ump likke always.
When game ova players drink champagne. No more white pants. I go get beer. Pants still clean.
Next Sunday no go polo game. I go fish.

Polo boss one Haole but look likke Mexican. Play good but no fall off horse. Hair on face for scare other player?

Pohi

MOKI'S LAWS

1. If at first you don't succeed- give up.

2. Early to bed and early to rise - and miss all the fun.

3. Eat, drink and be merry and get fat, drunk and happy.

4. If God helps them that help themselves - who helps them that don't?

5. If two's company and three's a crowd - is four a mob?

6. Don't look a gift horse in the mouth - it might bite you.

7. If the early bird catches the worm - stay in bed.

8. Happiness is the winner in the game of life!

The Life Of
Michael C. Butler
In His Own Words

If you're not living
life on the edge,
you're taking up
too much room.

Note: Publish date yet to be established

MOKI and MICHAEL BUTLER

Moki, the eloquent polo horse, is indeed me, with a tale involving my boss's son, Mike, and his longtime friend, Michael Butler. Michael, an intriguing and accomplished individual who nicknamed Mike 'Baby Bear'. Michael recently left us. He was a frequent visitor to the Sandwich Isles, often a guest in the home of Murph, Moki's favorite rider, person and Lady.

You might recall seeing Michael Butler play a few times, but Fred always kept him from playing chukkers on me. One of the sad deprecations in his otherwise fine life.

Michael was a visionary, who broke all the rules of Broadway musical theater to produce 'HAIR, ' where the cast wears the same amount of clothing that Moki wears at pasture. In addition to my Mike, Michael Butler was friends with John Kennedy, Rock Hudson, and many other celebrities.

Michael's friends have put together a biography book. While Moki's library is minimal, the book promises to be an outrageous and fascinating read. Michael always said: "if you were not living on the edge, you're taking up too much space."

More on Rewald

https://en.wikipedia.org/wiki/Ron_Rewald

"SIMPLE" INTEREST

When Moki inquired about Mr. Ron Rewald's predicament, the Boss explained, "Moki, Rewald was caught up in a scheme that's been around since the days of Ponzi."

He elaborated, "Here's how it works: You take a dollar from a friend and promise to invest it for them. Then, a few weeks later, you give them back two dollars. Naturally, your friend thinks you're a financial wizard and entrusts you with more money. So, you return four dollars to them. Now, you're hailed as a genius, and word spreads. Soon, everyone wants a piece of the action."

"As the money rolls in, you start living lavishly. You keep taking in funds, trying to outpace the returns. But eventually, the well runs dry. Suddenly, everyone demands their money back, and there's nothing left to give."

"In the end, the law catches up with you, and you find yourself behind bars. But, hey, think of the good times you had while you were living the high life - Buying the Hawaii Polo, club having a string orchestra play between chukkers, and wild women and booze."

Note: Rewald ended up serving time in Federal Prison..

MOKI QUOTE

"In my world, everyone's a pony and they all eat
rainbows and poop butterflies!" —

Dr. Seuss & Victoria

POLO HUMOR

An infamous nine goal polo player, Sean Monahan, dies and is sent to hell. Sean arrives at the main deck of hell and meets the devil.

The devil gives Sean a VIP escort. They enter an enormous dark red elevator and slowly descend past the various levels of hell. Each all designed to punish sybaritic behavior such as Sean's.

Large doors open at the lowest level and behold there is a club with over 10,000 acres of manicured polo fields. Sean Monahan exclaims : "Carrummba!! This is awesome!"

The devil shows Sean the sidelines. There are over 200 Argentine thoroughbred horses at the ready. Each horse is equipped with the finest Barnsby saddles and tack. Off to the side, there are several hundred polo mallets from Casa Villamil from the Argentine.

Standing alongside are some of the greatest polo players; all with 8,9 or 10 goal handicaps .

Sean, clearly, is dazzled. He mounts a horse and takes a few flawless turns and stops.

The Devil then hands a mallet to Sean, he makes a couple of circles and takes a few swings over the perfect grass. Sean looks at the Devil and yells: "Toss in a ball!"

The Devil smiles and says "Sean, now you know .... the hell of it."

Black Tie Barefoot Video QR

You Tube: **Black Tie Barefoot 2929**

MOKI and BLACK TIE-BARE FOOT

In the Sandwich Isles, Fred Daley forged a polo dynasty and a circle of enduring friendships, marked by remarkable events such as the Black-Tie Barefoot Event at the Marine Corps base in Kaneohe. During this memorable occasion, my dearest Murph was escorted by her son, Michael, alongside around 200 guests. They were celebrating the San Francisco Polo Team's triumph at the Honolulu Polo Club in Waimanalo.

The following day, while Murph treated me to carrots, she recounted the extraordinary festivities. A submarine dropped a diver offshore to present a special award to Marvin Silverman, a standout Windjammer Executive. The highlight of the evening involved each polo player giving Murph a strand of Pikakes. The first lei was bestowed by Bob MacGregor, and the last five leis were presented by Murph's son, Michael. Amidst numerous kisses, flowers, and an abundance of aloha spirit, it was a night to remember. My boss, Fred, observed the proceedings as a heavenly voyeur, thoroughly enjoying the spectacle.

Team San Francisco: Sean MacLeod, Randy Russell, Rich Arnold and their Irish Captain.

If you do nothing else while galloping down the polo field, try thinking."

Juan Carlos Harriott   Argentine Open 1977

As told by Argentine Open Winner nine goal Billy Linfoot

A glimpse of Eldorado and it's cage can be seen in the attached video created when Laura was 10 for her Grandmother at Christmas.

Tour of Donegal Farms with
P.T. Brent and Daughter, Laura

DONEGAL SHUFFLE

Perked up my ears when overhearing the visitors from San Francisco and Eldorado discussing the Donegal Shuffle created by Bill Meeker. The idea of the Donegal Shuffle intrigued me sensing it could be a valuable addition to training routines. Then came the rest of the story….

Here's how the action goes... two players each with their mallet and one ball race from one end of the polo pitch to the other end, the first one scoring, wins the round. The goal is to win three out of five.

It is a good test because you must judge the progress of the other horse. It simulates part of the game action with some reality. Imagine doing this for hours at a time, using different horses to challenge and embarrass your friends.

It's best to play this game with a trusted gentleman player. I'll tell you why!

During the first Shuffle between Bill Meeker and P.T. Brent played at Eldorado Polo Club in California, they each had their own ball in a 300-yard race to score. On the second run down the field Bill 's ball took an errant hop and he missed his ball. Rather than chase it, Bill immediately rode over to P.T.'s rear side - vigorously reached across his backside and foul hooked his mallet.

P.T.'s heart skipped a beat in complete shock – turning to Bill and said "HEY! What are you doing? With an Irish smile Bill said, "I forgot to tell you NO RULES."

Lesson from MOKI – **Don't forget the "gentleman" part…….**

Hypocrisy is not a way of getting back to the moral high ground.

"The only vice that cannot be forgiven is hypocrisy. The repentance of a hypocrite is itself hypocrisy."

– William Hazlitt

REUBEN & HYPOCRISY

Moki's good friend, Reuben Gracida, is from Santa Barbara. Reuben, an avid polo player, stands out not only for his skills on the field but also for his relaxed demeanor and gentlemanly conduct. His love for ocean swimming adds an adventurous touch to his personality.

In the world of polo, an interesting observation has been made about people's behavior. Some individuals reveal their 'dual' personalities; not during the game, but rather when they dismount and catch their breath. The intensity and competitiveness of polo can bring out different facets of one's character.

While many successful individuals in the sport maintain a level-headed approach, there are instances where some might harbor feelings of revenge if they perceive others not adhering to their expectations. The result is, in the heat of combat or lively polo game, the real personality is revealed as they have no time to hide it.

The dynamics of human behavior in the realm of polo add an intriguing layer to the sport, showcasing the varied aspects of individuals both on and off the field.

Far, Far better for an errant strike of the ball to hit a wooden horse than Moki's tender legs.

There are 2 hidden acronyms for Polo terms in the above drawing. Did you see them?

Team Donegall Mallets shown in picture on next page Called 'Sticks - aka Tacos' (in Argentina) Source; **World Famous Argentine Casa Villamil** polo mallets are made of previously selected and cured rattan cane (bamboo).

POLO HITTING CAGE

Moki : "There's a good reason why horses have big ears.". Also heard the folks from Donegal Farms talking about the Polo Cage. Didn't sound very good thinking it was for us ponies. Rolling my ears forward, learned it was actually a training program. The idea of a Polo cage seemed appealing, offering a controlled environment for practice and refinement of skills.

One of the players from the West Coast once said, ..."Practice on your offside - the left side if you are right-handed. Tennis players can return a ball from the side it is on, left or right. Same with polo."

Thought about the potential benefits of incorporating such training techniques. Despite not having one yet, Moki remained optimistic, especially with the hope that Fred's great-grandson, Ikua, might take the initiative to bring this idea to fruition, envisioning a future where the addition of these training elements would contribute to an even more dynamic and skill-enhancing polo experience.

Al Lopaka – Welcome to My World
Youtube.com

MOKI MISSES AL

Moki wants to share adventures with you. Life, much like the sport of polo, isn't always a gallop through rainbows and carrots. It holds an exhilarating charm, despite its inherent dangers. One of my dearest friends, Al Lopaka, a celebrated Hawaiian singer from Lanai, the Pineapple Isle, shares a special connection with Moki.

In a moment of keen observation, Moki noticed the wear and tear on Al's helmet, a testament to his daring experiences in the polo arena. In response, we ensured he received a sturdier, safer helmet after a particularly perilous incident that led to a coma. Sadly, we lost Al, someone dear, during that challenging time.

Moki often shows people Al Lopaka's old helmet, which offered him little protection. It's been out in the barn with me for a long time, unused. Moki looks at it and wishes Al was back another day to sing us some songs. It can't be said enough how important one's equipment is. Not using face masks or guards is a vanity issue. Face guards protect your eyes and your face and should be used. There is an old saying: "If you have a $10 head, buy a ten-dollar helmet."

In acknowledging the ups and downs of our journey, I extend my admiration to those who persist in their passion for polo and beyond. Life's path may have its share of somber moments, but it's the camaraderie and shared tales that make it a worthwhile ride.

"Scarlett was a one in a million and I miss her each and every day. I was so blessed to be able to provide for her during her later years. I thank you for bringing her to the island so I had that opportunity in my lifetime of having her."

Debi Dailey Hoffman

Laura with her horse Blackie, a gift from the late William Meeker.

MOKI's LOST PALS

In Moki's vibrant world, there are several other polo ponies and horses, but two of my best friends' hail from Donegal Farms, a 'beeg Island' known as America. They are Evita and Scarlett. These companions were the cream of the crop, and we formed an inseparable bond. Originating from an Irish culture, they found great comfort here, given that my boss and our First Lady, Murph, also shared Irish roots. Carrots were a universal favorite among us.

A young lady named Laura, who grew up at Donegal Farms, would occasionally come out to ride, and she never forgot to bring some delicious carrots for us. Moki and Laura shared a special fondness for Evita, the Argentine Mare, who once played the hero in a dramatic runaway episode that unfolded long ago.

Among our cherished companions was Scarlett, a beauty adorned with a white blaze and four white socks. She received love from many, especially Debi Dailey-Hoffman, who proffered a touching tribute and grave marker, she rests with honors near the Mokuleia Polo Club.

 She had some really good days toward the end of her journey and they bring a smile. She got so arthritic that standing to have her feet trimmed was difficult. Debi found a farrier that would work with her. Scarlett was in the habit of laying down for a nap at around 10:30 am, would nap for no less than 2 hours. When her toes needed trimming, our farrier would arrange his schedule to be there during her nap time. He would lay on the ground with her and clean and trim her feet.

It's easy for me to recognize wonderful horses but I want everyone to know I also have seen some very special people in the world in the love and the caring for us horses.

FRED

& MURPH

AND GOOD FRIENDS

FERN PIETSCH AND JOHN SPERLING

MOKI'S BOSS

My boss, a remarkable individual, is a United States Army Major and Purple Heart recipient who ventured into the world of polo, playing his first match at the Armory in Chicago's Lakefront. The military background adds a unique dimension to his polo journey. However, the Army emphasizes that polo should not consume one's entire life, urging individuals not to neglect their families and other valuable aspects of life. Supporting your family and taking care of them, whether it's the army or civilian life, has got to be paramount. Polo is a recreation sport and should NOT be all consuming. Learn to RIDE properly and how to treat a great horse, like Moki.

"Learn to ride ... become a "horseman." It's never too late! Many polo players do not ride well. Warm your horse up & down before and after each chukker. Polo is just like business, war and romance. You should allow time for its challenges." From the book: POLO 29, Chapter II

The paragraph highlights a challenge encountered during matches – visiting players and some home team members who lack proper riding skills. While Moki possesses an impressive physique, it becomes a bit challenging when interacting with players unfamiliar with the nuances of riding. Some struggle to maintain a trot, resembling a bouncing sack of garbage in their attempts. It's a humorous yet frustrating aspect of the game, emphasizing the importance of riders honing their skills.

Friend and Polo Player Bob MacGregor said,

"If you play polo, it's not a

matter of _if_ you get hurt,

it's _when_ you get hurt."

BOOS and RULES

My boss, Fred, has always been a firm believer in the importance of following the rules in polo. He emphasizes that actions deemed dangerous in front of the goal should warrant a penalty, adhering to the principle of safety first. However, he has observed a trend where umpires might prioritize popularity over enforcing necessary penalties, a practice he deems foolish. Fred firmly believes in upholding the rules to keep everyone safe on the field.

Moki, being the observant horse that she is, has noticed the impact of good umpires on the game. A skilled umpire sets the tone right from the beginning, making it clear that they will enforce the rules diligently. When my boss umpires the game, players show respect. Clearly, with my boss, they are not prima donnas because they have a large net worth and can afford the best horses. Moki will never forget one time when my boss said to them when they were upset with a call, "Next Monday morning will write to the USPA and submit the ruling to arbitration."

It was a sublime statement of what will never occur; however, it calms people down. This proactive approach keeps all players on their toes, fostering an environment where everyone is aware that rules will be enforced, contributing to a safer and more enjoyable game.

Moki was never ridden by Bob McGregor, but he is a heck of a guy. He brought some visitors like Alexander Anolik and others from San Francisco who always bring a team adorned in pink shirts. Al Lopaka used to get up on the microphone, humorously declaring they were from San Francisco and in pink, playfully making them all blush.

Bob McGregor,.... with his wisdom :

Polo – Our sport has it all
GLAMOUR, STYLE, DANGER, and SPEED.

Sean MacLeod   **Murph Dailey**   **Michael Dailey**

Humm, are those REAL bowties?

MOKI and PIKAKES

Moki has a delightful story to share about the enchanting world of Hawaii Polo and its most beloved lady, the 'First Lady of Hawaii Polo,' Elizabeth Murphy Dailey. When she and Fred arrived in town, their presence transformed not only the hotel business but also the realm of polo. Their first order of business was welcoming a horse named Moki into their lives, a horse who adored Murph more than sugar cubes and apples. Murph, in turn, rode me nearly every day, creating a bond that echoed through the polo fields.

Every year on their anniversary, Fred would gift Murph a Lei made of multiple strands of Pikakes, the most exquisite and delicate flowers in Hawaii. Each strand represented a year of their marriage. You can find these beautiful Pikakes at the Cindy Flower Lei Store on Maunakea Street. Unfortunately, horses, even a celebrity 'Author Horse', aren't allowed inside. Despite that, my dearest Murph would be adorned with so many Pikakes that she could barely breathe, enveloped in a captivating fragrance. Everyone admired her, but none more than her cherished polo companion, Moki.

**Rebecca
& Mike Dailey**

The young "Becca" MISS VIRGINIA

MOKI and BECCA

There is a special place in my heart for Becca Dailey, a remarkable rookie polo player and Michael's wonderful wife, who's also a devoted mother to their two incredible children, Devon and Mariah.

Moki still remembers the joy on her face in that cherished photo, wearing her Oxley polo helmet, proudly displayed near my stall in the barn. It captured one of her first chukkers, her smile beaming from ear to ear, radiating pure happiness. After years of admiration, Becca finally embraced polo, and her infectious enthusiasm made us all immensely proud.

My fondness for Becca traces back to the early days when she first crossed paths with a young Michael Dailey at the Santa Barbara Polo Club. It seems like a lifetime ago now, but her presence nearby has always been a comforting constant for me.

As Moki reflects on these memories, she can't help but feel a sense of warmth and gratitude for the wonderful connections that enrich our lives.

THE

DAILEY

FAMILY

FRED and MURPH
Plus MIKE
And More

Including
Stories and excerpts from MEMORIES
By Fred Dailey

BEFORE MOKI

Moki can remember nothing before life with Fred and Murph. Certainly, they felt the same about me. So, in FRED'S own words, enjoy their stories in:

Editor's note: The book MEMORIES by Fred Dailey is a wonderful read detailing the many events of an American hero and entrepreneur. (Available on Amazon.)

We have included many pages and/or excerpts directly from the book where space allowed. When it was necessary to skip multiple pages or paragraphs you will see * * *. *Italic type denotes editors' choice to include just a brief synopsis of the events in other in-between skipped pages.*

"... A tall good-looking officer walked through the place like he owned it; later he sent a note over to me. The rest is history!"

Elizabeth Murphy
09 December 2013

I MEET "MURPH"

Shortly after the year-end, I received orders to leave Tanforan and report to Sacramento, headquarters of the 4th Air Force. After a few weeks in this permanent Army post and a new course of indoctrination, I was posted to a P-38 Air Base at Santa Maria, California, as C.O. of the overseas training squadron. Here, with another promotion, I wound up as probably the most hated Captain in Santa Maria as my command shoved each young pilot and ground crew through a tough course of physical and ground combat training.

For the first time since flight school, these "crushed hat kids" were forced to do something besides fly an airplane and sit around the Officers Club drinking beer. They rose and shone at dawn, ran obstacle courses, learned to use firearms and in general learned how to stay alive among the enemy, if shot down from the "wild blue yonder". There were a great deal fewer of them at night in the restaurants and bars of Santa Maria after a day of absorbing the combat course in addition to their hours of flight training.

Eventually, as air group after air group moved through final stages at Santa Maria and left for overseas, the ground combat training program became more acceptable to pilots and crews - especially as word filtered back from combat areas. My assistants and myself finally fell into an organized routine that gave us time to occasionally leave the base for an evening in Santa Maria. It was on one of these evenings that an officer and friend entered a local restaurant with a young lady on his arm that immediately caught my attention.

As this manuscript makes no pretention as a contribution to great literature, but is more a matter of simple reporting, probably of interest only to a few relatives at a later date, I will not try to put into words the emotional impact of what was to follow....

At any rate, something electric took place as they say in the paperbacks, and the next day a phone call was made that changed two lives.

Murph, as I learned she was called, was a laboratory technician in the Santa Maria civilian hospital. Then twenty four years old, she was a member of a strong Catholic family and a scholarship graduate of Mount St. Mary's College in Los Angeles; a lovely, fun-filled, green-eyed, black-haired colleen, with brains as well as charm. After my phone call and our first date and several that followed, we both must have known that regardless of my age and marital problems and her own strong Catholic background, there was no way for our future, if any, not to be joined when this war ended. For the next few months we were together whenever her work and my duties made it possible.

During this period a young pilot was assigned to my unit as a liaison officer between my training command and the 4th Air Force headquarters in Sacramento. His job was to fly others and myself back and forth to headquarters whenever necessary.

Second Lieutenant Marvin Taylor was persuaded (ordered?) by me to escort Murph's visiting sister to the Officer's Club dinner one evening in Santa Maria. A wartime romance began and an eventual marriage. Marv would later become my brother-in-law. We lost track of each other during the rest of the war years as Marv covered his chest with medals flying fighter aircraft in Italy and Europe.

A few days after leaving the hospital my orders were to Salt Lake City. There to meet me were Marv and his new bride-Murph's sister Kat, and Murph, who had transferred to the Salt Lake hospital.

Several weeks later, my desire to serve overseas instead of being a home-based training officer was realized – I was headed to Washington D.C for overseas duty.

Now came the difficult part, leaving dear Murph. She, too, felt that after those few happy months at Santa Maria, a change in her own life would make things easier. She decided to leave Santa Maria and take a position in a laboratory in Los Angeles. And so the two of us prepared to part with only the hope that someday we'd be together again.

"By all means, marry. If you get a good wife you'll become happy; if you get a bad one, you'll become a philosopher."

SOCRATES

12 SEPTEMBER 1980

MURPH AND I "GET HITCHED"

In Denver several weeks were spent while the ears were treated and where both malaria and dengue were diagnosed. Nothing much in those days could be done for the fevers other than large doses of Quinine and Atabrine, which later was found to be useful only to turn one's skin yellow.

Discharged from the Denver hospital, I was then flown to an Army hospital in Miami, Florida for additional treatment.

In the meantime, my divorce was finalized and I was anxious to leave the Army and resume life as a civilian. Eventually in June 1946 in Atlanta, Georgia, I was discharged from the armed service and transferred to the Reserves with the rank of Major, a hearing aid (never used), a few commendations and war medals and four years of memories.

Murph and I were married in June 1946 in Atlanta. An amusing item about our marriage that we will always remember:

To procure the usual licenses for prospective husband and wife, we visited the Atlanta courthouse and lined up to pay a five-dollar fee at a cashier's window marked "Marriages." Adjacent to this window was another similar window marked "Divorces." Upon our departure after making the five-dollar marriage license deposit, cashiers in both windows gave us the usual Georgia farewell to departing guests, "Hurry back now". Although relieved from active duty in Atlanta and assigned to the Army Reserve, I was again ordered to return to Florida for hospitalization shortly after Murph and I were married. With returning bouts of malaria and dengue fever, plus the infected eardrum and a partially useless right arm, I was not allowed to leave Miami Beach. Here the former Coral Gables Hotel had been converted to a general hospital for combat wounded and though the luxurious gardens and even a swimming pool were a change from the usual Army infirmary, it was still the same old Army life with most ambulatory patients anxious to leave and become civilians again.

* * * *

Eventually, after numerous tests and examinations, I was allowed to leave the hospital with a disability record for which I have received a small monthly pension check throughout the years.

As Murph had heard a lot about my pre-war trips to Cuba, we decided to spend a few days there before leaving for California.

Havana before Castro was a tourist-fun city. Now that  the war was over, it was again full of foreign visitors enjoying the open gambling, nightclubs, and other tourist traps. As I was still in uniform, we were given every courtesy and assistance and had no problem in getting a room at the Hotel National, which, although expensive for us, was considered the finest in the city.

We enjoyed seeing the sights of old Havana, the El Marro Fort and Morro Bay, and in the evening strolled the streets where it seemed in front of every restaurant there was a band playing. A gathering place for U.S. tourists was Sloppy Joe's Bar. Here we frequently enjoyed their famous daiquiris and had our photographs taken with the aid of an old-fashioned camera wielded by their photographer using a hand-held trough containing gunpowder for the flash.

We also had a visitor. Harry Fontaine, my erstwhile roommate, had decided to join our honeymoon by simply walking away from the hospital and boarding a plane to Havana, where he also checked into our hotel and notified us of his arrival. Three on a honeymoon would normally seem strange, but with Harry's command of Spanish and his contacts with the local press, we found ourselves having a wonderful time and meeting a number of locals who made it their business to see that the newly-weds had a good time in Cuba. Among these were the Domeq Brothers, producers of rum products, who gave a party for us in their penthouse atop the rum factory.

All good things coming to an end, Murph and I finally bid goodbye to our Cuban friends and to Harry, who having already been A.W.O.L. for a week, decided to spend a few more days in Cuba. Whatever discipline the Army may have taken with Harry, he never let us know, although he eventually returned to his New York newspaper work and we kept in correspondence for a number of years.

Murph and I took up residence in California. Murph landed a position in a laboratory, and I a position with a trailer manufacturing association.

This was my start in the construction and development business.

****

TELESCOPE: **Michael Kama'aina Dailey**
The prospective parents, however, after doing some arithmetic, felt
the pending newborn should be either "Super Chief"
or "Super Chieftess depending on gender.
Mama and Papa Bear 13 November 1952

On or about 1952, we began to think about retirement and some world travel.

We left for New York City by rail on the **Super Chief** February 1952 to embark for France on the SS Ile de France. The name "Super Chief" and the date are important to keep in mind due to later events in history.

We had planned to spend at least a year in Europe. beginning with some time in Paris. *Ready to see the rest of Europe we purchased a small British two-seater roadster.****

Our odyssey included the south of France, Switzerland, Italy, and Spain. Spain was our favorite. Even had our little car hoisted aboard a steamer and visited Gibraltar and North Africa. Returning to Spain strange things started to happen.

Murph had always been in the best of health with an appetite only surpassed by my own, started toying with her food. *Suddenly, in Spain, the smell of olive oil became obnoxious. Eventually, it occurred to us that Mother Nature had more things in store for us than a year in Europe.*

Found an English-speaking doctor in Switzerland that confirmed out own guesswork and set the date of the new arrival to the Dailey family in November. After doing some arithmetic, felt the newborn Super Chief or Chiefess. *We did stay several more months to see as much as we could until it was time to settle down.*

We had many discussions about where to spend the future years now that there would be more than the two of us. ***

Eventually we settled on Hawaii for its near perfect climate, its friendly people, and the fact that was a US Territory.

THE Waikikian
HAWAII'S MOST BEAUTIFUL HOTEL

The WAIKIKIAN, located on Waikiki's lagoon and beach, captures the romance of early Polynesia yet offers every modern convenience and service. The WAIKIKIAN'S low rambling buildings and handsome new annex express the Hawaii of your dreams. In the WAIKIKIAN each room and suite is completely private and affords either an ocean or mountain view. You may swim from the WAIKIKIAN'S own private beach in a crystal lagoon, in the huge fresh water pool, or in the famous Waikiki surf on the open sea beach beyond. The beach boys will arrange your catamaran or outrigger rides, surfing, or water skiing.

Cocktails will be served on your own private lanai at sunset in the gay Papeete Bar—or around the pool. You will dine in the languid beauty of tropical nights facing the open beach on the Tahitian Lanai to soft music of the South Seas. At twilight you will be serenaded by native singers during the impressive ancient ceremony of lighting the Kahili torches in the Tiki Garden.

You will find your fondest dreams of South Sea paradise come true at the WAIKIKIAN.

WAIKIKIAN HOTEL - WAIKIKI

TAHITIAN LANAI

EXOTIC COCKTAILS

papeete bar

ALL THE GAYETY AND
ABANDON OF THE OLD TAHITI

THE WAIKIKIAN 1956

Although I had no experience in hotel operation other than our visits when traveling, it seemed to me that the hotel business, like any other, was simply a matter of the application of good business methods for success. Little did I know that hotel management is an exacting and technical profession.

We were fortunate in picking a field of business that was on the verge of tremendous expansion, as the war-weary world began to become conscious of the importance of vacations and the enjoyment of life. The more we studied hotels and what made them tick, the more we realized that we should build something different in a first-class quality to ensure not only a successful financial venture but have a hell of a lot of fun in the meantime.

We assumed we could go to the banks and financial firms and obtain construction loans much as we had done with our houses. The turndowns by these respected institutions, while surprising to us, were unanimous. They simply did not make loans to hotels, as they were considered too speculative.

Rather than give up...we sold stock to friends. Eventually with enough stock sold, we were able to finance the construction of eighty bedrooms, a restaurant and lobby. We named the hotel the WAIKIKIAN. When completed, it was unusual enough in design to make a considerable splash with travel agents and tourists to be moderately successful in its first year.

During the first few years of the hotel operation, we began to learn a few things about Hawaii and its past and the turn around of the labor situation from its pre-war exploitation by the plantation owners and haole (Caucasian) families to its opposite extreme.

Now organized labor took over and life became miserabl
for all of us during the strife-torn years of strikes on one sid
and the fear of Communism on the other. Those of us livin
in the islands at that time will never forget the weeks of th
shipping strike when food staples were limited and alon
with that the tourists simply stopped traveling to the islands

Eventually the labor wars settled down and th
Waikikian and other hotels began to prosper, only to no
find the Waikikian targeted by the labor organizations.

We realized that the only way we could compete wit
the big hotels with their million-dollar advertising program
was to develop a reputation for personal service. Part o
our strategy included setting up an employee profit-sharin
plan (the first in Hawaii hotels) to form a partnershi
between the employees and us. Additionally, we pai
approximately the same wages as other hotels. As a resul
when the union organizers went to work on our staff, the
had little to sell to them except payment of union dues. Th
official labor board called an election and the result was th
90% of our employees voted against union organization.

The choice of our people regarding union organizatic
had one peculiar result. The Tahitian Lanai restaura
began to become the luncheon meeting place for unic
chiefs and their associates.

We could only conclude that perhaps these unic
bigwigs preferred to convene in a non-union restaurant
order to avoid their own rank and file. At any rat
their practice of meeting at our hotel continued througho
the years – and – remained union free.

With rooms, grounds, and buildings in a tropic
atmosphere, the Waikikian gradually became know
as a unique and select place to spend a vacation.

The lobby building with its hyperbolic-parabolo
construction became one of the most photographed buildings
Hawaii.

Almost by accident, we stumbled upon a policy of protecting guests from publicity rather than exploiting those who were famous in the press and media. As a result many well-known personages from Hollywood stars to members of royal families chose the Waikikian when seeking a private hideaway.

We were also the only hotel owning a concert grand piano. As a result we hosted every visiting pianist in our "Musical Suite." The list of artists who practiced at the Waikikian for the ensuing twenty years was a "Who's Who" of the concert world.

In our third year we were financially able to build additional suites and rooms on adjacent land, bringing the total of accommodations to nearly three hundred persons. We were also able to employ a high-salaried and well-experienced manager who took over most of the daily burden of operation, leaving Murph and me free to concentrate on making our hotel well known around the world..

We joined a group of some of the world's finest independently owned hotels together in advertising and exchange of guest referrals. It was through this group that we met many of the fraternity of owners and managers, who on our future travel around the world made such travel for us a delight due to the VIP treatment we received.

　　* * * *

A LETTER FROM LONDON

It all started with a cable we received on

July 6, from England:

> "The Queen and the Duke of Edinburgh have commanded the Lord Chamberlain to invite Mr. and Mrs. Fred Dailey to the marriage of The Prince of Wales and The Lady Diana Spencer in St. Paul's Cathedral at 11:00 A.M. on Wednesday, 29 July. The Lord Chamberlain would be pleased to learn by return whether they are able to be present.
>
> If attending please advise an address in London to which admission cards may be sent."
>
> Signed, "Lord Chamberlain."

Obviously, with Murph's Irish background, there was only one answer...YES... and so we cabled we would attend and began to make our plans.

Wondering why we had been so fortunate to receive such an invitation, we decided that it was possibly triggered by several past events in Fred's life. The first was the fact that he had trained under Lord Mountbatten during World War II with a commando group at Fort Meade, Maryland. Mountbatten was brought to the U.S. at that time to indoctrinate the unit with his experience as a commando in Norway. As this was a very small group, Fred got to know Mountbatten and kept up the acquaintance throughout the years.

In the fifties, Fred and Prince Philip, Charles' father, played polo together in England and then in the early seventies when Michael was playing quite well, he was selected as a member of the "Young America" team to play at Windsor against a team captained by Prince Charles. This furthered his acquaintance with Charles, and several years later when Charles visited Hawaii he was our houseguest and played polo at Mokuleia. In discussing the matter with some friends in England we were told that Prince Charles had a list of personal friends who were invited to the wedding. We didn't realize how highly prized these invitations were until we arrived in England and learned how the limited number of invitations were issued to conform with the maximum seating in St. Paul's. Murph and I were the only persons from Hawaii fortunate enough to be invited.

The next step was for us to shoot another cable to our friend Lord Patrick Beresford, asking him to find some possible accommodations. He immediately replied that he had arranged an apartment, or as they are called in England "a flat", for us in the central area of London, just a few blocks from Buckingham Palace in a section called Edgeton Gardens in a unit owned by Lady Astor.

Travel plans were made, and our friend Lord Beresford not only handled the accommodations, but assured us he would also make plans to help us with the appropriate attire for such Royal Occasions. This is not to say that Murph did not spend a fortune shopping in San Francisco before we left for England Several days of activities occurred before and after the wedding. The participation in all was grand.

Now the problem was, what do you send as a wedding gift to two people who already seem to have everything - crutches for Charles and a polo mallet for Diana?

The problem was solved as the friendship and correspondence with Prince Charles continued through the years and it is interesting to note that Charles would always take time from his busy days to send hand-written letters and notes, all of which we have kept for posterity. When their first child was born, Murph and I had a Hawaiian highchair made for their future polo player, which we shipped to them in 1982, receiving their thanks and an invitation to visit them in the future.

Then Prince Charles & Mike with 1974 hair

THE

DAILEY

FAMILY

PHOTOS

From "Hawaii Hospitality" Magazine
Annual Issue 1980-1981

Fred Dailey 1981

Following a career in design, construction and finance in California, Fred Dailey arrived in Honolulu in 1953 with retirement in mind, During his military service he had been billeted in Hawaii and planned then to return to paradise and enjoy the good life.

The old Niumalu Hotel, a bungalow hotel set in lush foliage, caught his fancy; and there was a strip of property available just adjacent to the hotel that had been the birthplace of Duke Kahanamoku. It sat neatly in the curve of the of Ala Moana Blvd. And the idea of a Polynesian hotel seemed to fit.

Next came the meeting of Fred Dailey and George "Pete" Wimberly and the hotel with the hyperbolic para-beloid was born. The Waikikian was open at the "gate way to Waikiki" in 1956.

During his tenure as president, the local hotel association chartered the Matson ship *Lurline* and a group of three hundred members, travel agents and tourism officials from Hawaii sailed away to Los Angeles and subsequently to San Francisco and Seattle.

A promotional and advertising program on Hawaii was presented to travel agents and related industry members in each city. During that time Dailey appeared on sixteen radio and television stations publicizing Hawaii with the current Miss Hawaii and other entertainers.

At that time, and today, Dailey advocates "quality tourism". He feels that "not enough attention is given to FITs (free independent traveler", and to upgrading plans for the visitor. "There is" he says, "too much emphasis on inexpensive, mass-produced tourism."

Daley, who was born in Auroa, Illinois, constructed and operated resorts in Southern California. After the opening of the Waikikian in Hawaii, he also developed the Driftwood Hotel and Mokuleia Beach Colony.

Organizer and president of the Hawaii Polo Club at Mokuleia, he has revived the sport that was once the fancy of King Kalakaua at Kapiolani Park. He is also a member of the Santa Barbara Polo Club and governor of the U.S. Polo Association and is instrumental in bringing clubs from Ireland, Britian (including Price Charles), Chile, Florida, California and the Philippines to highlight the five-month season.

He authored *Blood, Sweat, and Jears* and *One Man's Meat* and served during World War II in the China-Burma and South Pacific theaters as a U.S. Army Major, receiving the Purple Heart and commendation medals.

MURPH DAILEY

MURPH

First lady of Hawaii polo

Imagine it is 1952. You are in Hawaii standing on the dock at Aloha Tower, welcoming the SS Lurline. A remarkable couple are on the ship's bridge with the captain. Soft music from bygone days is playing as hula girls dance and island boys are diving into the harbor to collect coins tossed by passengers.

ALOOOHA! The hotel business, as well as polo life in Hawaii, would never be the same again. Why? This extraordinary lady (who picked up the moniker "Murph" during her medical years) and her husband had arrived to establish their home, and later polo, in the Sandwich Isles. They brought a way of life that Hawaii will treasure.

Those who believe they have visited polo in Hawaii during the last half-century and have not met Murph may have missed the boat! If you do meet her, be assured she will ride away with your heart forever. Murph is a warm-hearted woman who makes everyone, regardless of his or her status, feel very special.

Winston Churchill once said polo is your passport to the world. Fred and Murph earned this passport. They have hosted the "who's who" of polo worldwide, including the Prince of Wales, the King of Malaysia, Marquis of Waterford, the Sultan of Brunei, the Maharajah of Jodhpur, the president of the Argentina Polo Association, 10-goaler Memo Gracida and players from every corner of the globe.

Fred was Mister Polo in Hawaii. He ran the Hawaii Polo Club, a great club, but as an ex-army officer he was disciplined. After practice chukkers, prior to Sunday's big games, Fred would give a no-nonsense talk. His affluent members, who were the top corporate men of Hawaii as well as some veteran horsemen, were all lined up. Fred laid down the Sunday protocols such as blue blazers, club ascots, and polo gear placed on display for the spectators. These power men loved the game; albeit they suffered through Fred's lectures. Right at the end of the sermon along came Murph with a basket of warm chocolate chip cookies. They were a great team.

Since they met during World War II, Murph and her late husband Fred's history reads like a great American novel. In fact, it is and has been vividly captured in one of Fred's two books, "Memories," which is a must read for nostalgic polo fans as well as anyone who appreciates a good love story.

Elizabeth Murphy was a graduate pharmacist as well as preordained to be a doctor during World War II. However, her life took a dramatic detour when a self-confident army officer crashed into a wartime officer's club and boldly interrupted Murph and her date. This became quite a moment, thus launching chapter one of this American love story, the real McCoy.

Murph was a brilliant designer. She also handled a fly rod nicely, played a fair game of polo, and was a serious hiker. In fact, Murph was no slacker on the polo pitch; she has ridden out and taught some humility to more than few beginners, such as this author. (She was also the first woman to be granted membership in the USPA after World War II.)

Murph's devotion and love for her son Michael is well known. She lives on the ocean contiguous to the polo club with son Mike, his wife Becca and their children Devon and Mariah. She now has her first great-grandchild, a cutie named Isla. Her family members all have homes nearby.

If you are headed to the Hawaiian Isles, be sure not to miss Sunday polo at Mokuleia and give a warm *aloha nui loa* to Murph. She will likely tell you, "Keep your eye on the ball." She is at every Sunday game and is still a trim figure, dressed impeccably.

The handicap committee of the Hawaii Polo Club claims they have no members rated "10 Goals." Perhaps this committee should proffer the 10-goal rating to the beautiful lady in the front row.

This Irish colleen, who is the epitome of style and class, will reach the century mark by Christmas of 2018. One hundred, and she is still riding away with our hearts forever.

–Patrick T. Brent

So much more to come...........

Special Message from
Governor David Y. Ige
Presented to
Elizabeth "Murph" Dailey
December 9, 2018

It is my pleasure and honor to join your family and friends in wishing you a Happy 100th Birthday! You have reached an incredible milestone and a truly special one it is. Today is the beginning of another memorable year in your wonderful life.

As the first lady of Hawai'i polo, friends and family cherish you for your strength and spirit, warmth of your heart, and all that you do. No treasure can be compared to your love for people and polo. Enjoy every moment and every day with aloha.

Your 100 years have been filled with lots of laughter and love and many sweet memories. Elizabeth, I congratulate you on your 100th birthday and wish you continued good health and happiness.

With warmest regards,

David Y. Ige

DAVID Y. IGE
Governor, State of Hawai'i

QR FOR Murph
Party

Or you tube / Murph
Dailey 100 birthday

CELEBRATE 100

MURPH & IKUA

&

ONE

Saturday, December 8th, 4–8pm
Hawai'i Polo Club
RSVP: 808.637.4692

Happy 102nd Birthday
MURPH DAILEY!

TARTUFO KID
with Friends &
Family

DATELINE: AUXILIARY FIELD
HAWAII POLO CLUB MOKULEIA
FRIDAY 07 MARCH 1976

"Murph" Dailey rides a rookie poloist

out of the action...

A treasured moment!

"And she rode away
with my heart forever."
Anonymous   07 March 1976

Eulogy for Murph by P.T. Brent

ALOHA MURPH
9 December 1918 – 3 May 2023

Elizabeth 'Murph' Dailey, a remarkable soul who graced this world with her presence.

Located at the longtime residence she and Fred Daily built at Mokuleia, 'Murph' gently faded away with her son, Michael and her daughter-in-law Amanda holding her hands. .

Murph was 104 years old. What a grand life she lived. She was born in Seattle, attended High School in Oxnard, and earned a scholarship to Mount Saint Mary's College in Los Angeles. Her ambitions of becoming a doctor were put on hold during World War II when she met and married the love of her life, Fred Dailey, an officer in the army.
They exchanged vows in Atlanta and embarked on a memorable honeymoon in Havana. Their son Michael was conceived on the Super Chief train, while hurtling across the vast expanse between Los Angeles and New York. Michael's arrival cemented the bonds of an extraordinary love story.
Ultimately arrived on the Lurline, where they launched the Waikikian Hotel and later the Hawaii Polo Club at Mokuleia. – yes, Murph played too.
Murph possessed an ethereal beauty, her eyes shimmering like emeralds, captivating all who had the privilege of meeting her. – she was a knockout. Was beloved by everyone she met.
Although her physical presence may have waned, the spirit of 'Murph' Dailey shall linger forever, a reminder of the beauty that graces our lives even in the face of the setting sun.

Murph is survived by her son Michael, his wife, Becca, her grandchildren, Devon and Mariah and their children Ikua, Isla, and Tadhg

Celebration of her life is scheduled for at the Hawaii Polo club at Mokuleia –On July 21, 2023, at 4PM

...

THE

DAILEY LEGACY

CONTINUES

The Equus
1696 Ala Moana Blvd, Honolulu HI 96815

• 1.808.949.0061 • 1.808.949.4906
• equushotel.com

Chamberlin Inn
1032 12th Street, Cody, Wyoming 82414

• 307-587-0202 • www.chamberlininn.com
• info@chamberlininn.com

Center: MIKE and wife, BECCA DAILEY

Far Left: Daughter MARIAH & husband Michael standing
                Right: Son DEVON & wife Amanda standing
"Starring" at stage right - with a smile to light the room-
MURPH

Devon is now the 3rd generation to continue the
family POLO empire.
Mariah lives in Ireland with her husband
and their son Tadhg.
Mike and **Becca** manage their hotel properties
in Honolulu and Cody, Wyoming.

DEVON with his pride and joy ...
ISLA & IKUA

Mariah with Tadhg

Dailey Family Secrets

WYOMING
FLAG

USA
FLAG

KYEOTB

ISLA
IKUA
Tadhg

IRISH
FLAG

HAWAIIAN FLAG   SHAMROCK

Did you find them without this help?
If not, go look for them again!

MOKI GOES TO COLLEGE

Polo College Introduction

02:42

Polo College is intended as a free source of Polo Knowledge. Through the combined efforts of some dedicated polo people, some who are no longer with us. Developed without cost to the polo association. In this new digital age it is now accessible vis a vis internet on Vimeo. Glamor, Style, Danger and speed. Ou great sport rates respect - respect for safety, respect for the horses, respect for each other and for our great sport. Let us not lose perspective of these values.

KYEOTB, from Hawaii

WELCOME to POLO COLLEGE

INTRODUCTION by DR. BOB WALTON
FORMER PRESIDENT, USPA

Https://vimeo.com/58000810

"Patrick Brent, experienced polo player, has produced a most informative "college" of the great sport of polo, available to all pro bono. Only Patrick has had the skill knowledge and the desire to put such a valuable production free to all."

Ambassador Glen Holden
President, International Federation of Polo (FIP)r

LESSONS

Moki's Polo College took me on a nostalgic journe
back to the 1980s, a time when my life revolve
heavily around Polo. I served as the governor of th
West Coast Circuit, the largest circuit in the USPA, an
was honored to be elected president of the Pol
Training Foundation (PTF). Today, the PTF hold
ownership of invaluable educational videos, thoug
sadly they aren't being disseminated as widely as the
should be.

Reflecting on my early days as a rookie player,
desperately craved the knowledge that Polo Colleg
now offers. Back then, resources were scarce – n
books, schools, or classes to turn to. If such a wealth
knowledge had been available, would have gladi
paid $10,000 for it.

Nowadays, there's a plethora of resources availabl
but none match the depth and breadth of Polo Colleg
These tutorials cover every aspect of Pol
supplemented by enlightening 'Round Tabl
discussions from across the globe.

"Knowledge is Power."

Moki understands the significance of these words.

LEGS WRAPS

By James Rice expert pro groom to ten goaler
Cecil Smith and the Butler family --- one unique gentleman. James
Rice was the long-time groom to the famous Butler
family who put much into our great sport including
the infamous Michael Butler. He groomed for
royalty and many high goalers in a long, very
professional career based out of Chicago Oakbrook
- WGC

vimeo.com//54559390

••

HITTING from Hawaii
Mike & Fred Dailey
The late Fred Daily
Mister Polo in the Hawaiian Islands
narrates as his 5-goal son demonstrates.
Oahu Hawaii

vimeo.com/54559388
••

HITTING
Joe Barry, the late, albeit legendary (9 goaler),
teaches hitting. Played all over the world.
Famous at scoring a goal from a mid-field
strike — 150 yards out -
and one fine gentleman

vimeo.com/54559387
••

FEEDING

Lessons - Feeding Polo Horses with Benny
Gutierrez
Benny Gutierrez and friend give the low
down.
The Equestrian diet has to be an athletic one.

vimeo.com/54559386

•••

BODY POSITION - STRIKING
BALL

Rege Ludwig - professor of polos second to
none Sawadee Kop Rege - and one fine gentleman
ptb Eldorado

Vimeo.com/54509639

•••

BITS WITH MIKE DAILEY

The importance of bits is critical. The right bit
will make a polo mount invaluable The wrong
one can do damage to both horse and rider.
Mokuleia, HI   pay attention

vimeo.com/54509637

•••

CHAT with WES LINFOOT
AND JAY CASSELL

In rare opportunity to chat with a member of the legendary polo family The Linfoots. Posted by Jay Cassell in Woodside California area circa: 1986

vimeo.com/54509634

POLO EQUIPMENT

by the Late Roland Hicks –
one darn good gent
- son of Harry Hicks an adventurer

vimeo.com/54582740•

SCHOOLING THE POLO PONY

By Johnny Gonzales -
Mack Jason's outstanding three goal pro for many years from Eldorado MCMLXXXVI

Vimeo.com/54582739

....

MALLETS

Mike and Fred Dailey
That's one of the best father-son
Legacy's in all the polo world

Vimeo.com/54582741
....

TAIL TYING   with the Dailey's

During the actual chuckers, the tail is
 tied so that the horse could not swish
it up and hook the mallet which would
cause an embarrassing moment, and
perhaps as well as dangerous one.

vimeo.com/54584878
....

VET CARE

Dr. Steve Carter a polo veteranarian
from the Eldorado Polo area discusses
purchasing a new horse for polo. His
model "Kipling" from the Donegal Farms
polo string. Trainor Kelly Nichols **1986**
circa: Donegal Farms --- MCMLXXXVI

vimeo.com/54584877
....

FOULS

Corky and Regi Linfoot polo experts second to none. Circa: Eldorado MCMLXXXVI.

vimeo.com/54565818

READING POLO LIBRARY

by Roland Hicks
The late Roland Hicks - one damn good guy share some good books to read MCMLXXXVI. His Dad Harry Hicks, two goaler --- built the Santa Barbara Polo Club.

vimeo.com/54582738

ROUND TABLES

Hawaii Polo Club
Murph Dailey Mike Dailey
Devon Dailey / Patrick Brent

Vimeo.com/54734090

....

South Florida Polo Coach House
Feb 15,2014   Wellington Fla

`   vimeo.com/116299719

....

Eldorado & Empire Polo Clubs
Filmed at Donegal Farms Indio Ca.
Camera by Duke Nolasco
Members attending: Patick Brent
Danny Scheraga – President PTF
Steve Lane – Head Umpire USPA
Glenn Hart - Oregon
Craig Ramsby – Wyoming Club
Manager

vimeo.com/54565816
....

ORCHIDS for POLO COLLEGE

Aloha Patrick, what an incredible contribution to our ancient passion, as we welcome this new polo venue we in Hawaii say, "Aloha a me e komo mai" Welcome come in and enjoy. ahui hou.

Allen Hoe, Honolulu Polo Club   Have a 10-Goal day!

Our club believes the round table emphasis on gentlemanly conduct on and off the field has been overlooked far too long - Polo College says exactly what needed to be said for a long time - time to comport ourselves with the style and form our world class sport has earned."

Mickey Brittan Founder Chairman Fair Hills Polo and Hunt Club 17 March 2013
A Video USPA Blue Book, style & class on the polo pitch, polo trivia & history and more.

It's great to see the website come to fruition. I believe it has a special message separate from instruction. Really like the concept of sportsmanship and camaraderie among the players. There is no question you hit a home run with the idea that the horses are the true athletes of our support and they deserve special protection and care.

Denny Geiler
USPA Pacific Coast Circuit Governor...... successor to a long line of governors - all gifted athletes and brilliant leaders of polo.

POLO 29 TRIVIA

1. Name the last polo player to legally play LEFT-HANDED - as he was grandfathered in until career ended.

2. Name the only native-born USA player to ever win the Argentine open??

3. Name the player who after long unthinkable prison by the Japanese in WWII and came back and went to a Ten Goal handicap?

4. What year did polo arrive in the USA?

5. How do you line up post a penalty one for a throw in...? bet we have you?

6. What was Mickey Brittan's handicap during his years with the United States Marine Corps and before he became a Beverly Hills/ Hollywood notable ??

7. What was the handicap of Bill Meeker during his Notre Dame football years??
- prior to shoving off for France and polo at Bagatelle ?

8. What mature fifty + lady player wiped out the author of this web site in his first chukker in Hawaii on 7 March 1976?

9. Is it true that polo players are smarter and better looking?

10. What is the origin of the word polo?

Answers ...... somewhere at the end of this book.

ANSWERS: POLO TRIVIA

1. Name the last polo player to legally play LEFT-HANDED / as he was USP' grandfathered in till career ended?   **Skee Johnson**

2. Name the only native-born USA player to ever win the Argentine open??
Billy Linfoot 9 goaler. Corky's Linfoot's father

3. Name the player who after long torturous imprisonment by the Japanese in WWII and came back and went to a Ten Goal handicap?
The imitable Robert Skene

4. What year did polo arrive in the USA? **Our centennial 1876**

5. How do you line up post a penalty one for a throw in...?bet we have you
**Yes we do! More penalty # one should be called -
now look it up in your blue book &reread the blue book
annually.**

6. What was Mickey Brittan's handicap during his years with the United States Marine Corps and before he became a Beverly Hills/ Hollywood notable ?? **8 (perhaps one of those U.S.M.C "Sea Stories")**

7. What was the handicap of Bill Meeker during his Notre Dame football years??- prior to shoving off for France and polo at Bagatelle ?   **Nine
Goals - blarney - no indeed, just the luck of the Irish**

8. What mature fifty + lady player wiped out/ rode off the author of this we' site in his first chukker ever in Hawaii on 7 March 1976?
Hawaii's incredible & lovable Mrs. Murph Dailey

9. Is it true that polo players are smarter and better looking?
Well.... don't ask this writer. He got a waiver.

10. What is the origin of the word polo?   **"pulu" f from the far
east / India a wood pulu from which the ball was made**

Did you win this trophy with all the correct answers?

Murph and the Irish Cup

The Equus

1696 Ala Moana Blvd, Honolulu HI 96815

• 1.808.949.0061 • 1.808.949.4906
• equushotel.com

Chamberlin Inn

1032 12th Street, Cody, Wyoming 82414

• 307-587-0202 • www.chamberlininn.com
• info@chamberlininn.com

MOKI

All good stories come to an end

n the changing tides of time, the essence of Fred, Murph, .nd myself, Moki, lingers just beyond the shore at Mokuleia, standing as a guardian presence over their herished ones. The tapestry of the Fred Dynasty continues ts march forward. The Boss's son, Michael, embraced a life f undeniable fortune, having chosen a woman named Rebecca—Becca—an ascent that defied all expectations. 'rom this union emerged two remarkable souls, Mariah and Devon, each contributing to the family's legacy.

And so, the lineage unfolds, cascading into the realms of the next generation. Mariah and Devon, in their turn, blessed he world with three radiant grandchildren—Isla, Ikua, and 'adhg (Timothy). The familial saga, an intricate narrative woven over time, speaks of love, resilience, and the nduring spirit that defines the Fred Dynasty.

n the silence of the Hawaiian breeze, whispers of tales merge, painting the canvas of this family's journey. Clearly, there are, at the very least, two great books written y me, Moki, chronicling the adventures, the joys, and the hallenges faced by this extraordinary family and their ircle of friends. The inked words will etch into the annals of nemory, ensuring that the legacy of Moki, the beloved Polo 'ony, remains indelibly imprinted on the hearts of those vho were fortunate enough to share in our story.

More books by Moki, Fred Dailey and PT Brent next page...........

MOKI

POLO IS A FOUR-LETTER WORD
MOKI's REVENGE

FRED DAILEY

- MEMORIES
- POLO IS A FOUR-LETTER WORD
- BLOOD, SWEAT AND JEERS**
- ONE MANS MEAT*
*World War II China-Burma & South Pacific
** WWII – available on AbeBooks.com

P.T.BRENT   (all)

A MARINE NAME MITCH – USMC
29 – An Anthology of Outrageous Stories
POLO 29
MOKI'S REVENGE (coauthor)
SEA 29 ALPHA
SEA 29 BRAVO
SEA 29 CHARLIE
SEA 29 TRILOGY COMPANION IV

Available on Amazon books

Made in the USA
Columbia, SC
27 August 2024

40376623R00080